Original title:
Life: A Series of Sighs and Surprises

Copyright © 2025 Creative Arts Management OÜ
All rights reserved.

Author: Victor Mercer
ISBN HARDBACK: 978-1-80566-138-2
ISBN PAPERBACK: 978-1-80566-433-8

The Balance of Hope and Doubt

Some days we laugh, some days we cry,
I dance with joy, then trip and sigh.
The coffee's strong, the toast is burned,
But hey, at least the lesson's learned!

A sock gone missing from the wash,
It tiptoes off, oh what a posh!
The cat, it plots my next big fall,
While dreaming grand, I hit the wall.

I plan my dreams with utmost flair,
Yet end up stuck in a comfy chair.
The surprises fly like wayward shouts,
Hope nests inside, while doubt just pouts.

So here we stand with joy and frown,
A smile for heights, a grin for down.
Through giggles shared and woes we chase,
In this funny game, we'll find our place.

The Sweet and Sour of Days

Some days start sweet as candy,
Yet others taste like bittersweet jam.
With every laugh, there's a mishap,
A sneeze in soup, oh what a slam!

Spilling coffee on a new white shirt,
And tripping over shoes in the hall.
We juggle work with giggles and grunts,
Life's a circus, we're just the brawl.

Underneath the Surface of Routine

Morning coffee, same old grind,
Yet a sock puppet steals the show.
Turns out your pet's quite the comedian,
Who knew the cat had such flow?

While brushing teeth, a song breaks out,
And dancing past the laundry pile.
Routine crumbles with every twist,
We tumble and laugh, for quite a while.

The Melody of Unforeseen Paths

Walking down a path so straight,
Oops! A puddle, a splash, a gasp!
Instead of grumbling, let's just sing,
A serenade with a clumsy clasp.

A wrong turn leads to joyful cheers,
Where ice cream trucks and laughter blend.
Adventures spring from silly slips,
What a way to meet a new friend!

Joy Sprouted from Rain

Raindrops tap like a playful tune,
Umbrellas spin, a waltz in grey.
With each drizzle, a dance erupts,
We leap in puddles, who needs the sun, hey?

Lightning strikes, yet we delight,
In muddy boots, we run and glide.
Every splash carries a giggle,
In storms, there's always joy to hide.

Sighs Sung Softly by the Soul

In moments of glee, I let out a sigh,
Like an out-of-tune bird taking flight in the sky.
Each chuckle a hiccup, a playful retreat,
As I stumble through humor, on my own two feet.

With winks and a nod, I dance with the breeze,
Tripping on laughter, oh, how it frees!
The world keeps spinning, but I take it slow,
Sighs sung softly, and the joy starts to grow.

Chasing Clouds of Yesterday

I chase the clouds that float on by,
As if they're ice cream cones in the sky.
Those fluffy memories, sweet and absurd,
Have me giggling like a confused little bird.

Running in circles, I leap and I bound,
Searching for treasures that cannot be found.
Each misstep, a tickle, each fall, quite a jest,
In this zany quest, I must confess!

One Foot in the Sun, One in the Rain

I stand with my sandals, feeling the heat,
While the other foot's splashed by a sprinkle so sweet.
Oh, should I be cheerful or confused in this game?
Sunshine and puddles both calling my name.

With socks soaked in laughter, I strut with a grin,
Life's comedic timing keeps pulling me in.
One foot in a puddle, the other in rays,
Dancing through moments in quirky arrays.

The Grains of Salt and Sweet

A sprinkle of salt in this sugar parade,
Adds flavor to the antics of choices I made.
With each tasty surprise that breezes my way,
The laughter gets louder, and worries decay.

I taste the confusion, a dash here, a swirl,
Savoring moments as they twirl and unfurl.
In a feast of the odd, I munch with delight,
Grains of joy scatter, and oh, what a sight!

Fleeting Glances at Tomorrow

Morning coffee, a wild affair,
Peanut butter caught in my hair.
Chasing dreams that never wait,
I trip on shoes that can't relate.

Plans drawn in the air, quite dense,
Why did I think that made sense?
With every step, a twist or turn,
Sometimes, I feel the world will burn.

The Art of Unplanned Awakenings

Alarm rings bright, I hit the snooze,
Forgot my pants, just in my shoes.
Breakfast calls but I cannot hear,
Chasing crumbs like a secret deer.

Sudden calls, actions unplanned,
A dance-off starts where I had planned.
Coffee spills, a joyful mess,
Who needs neatness? I'm blessed, I guess.

Echoes in the Chamber of Days

Yesterday's plans now scattered like cheese,
Thoughts fly by with the greatest of ease.
Laughter bubbles in the mundane,
Why do I give the cat my name?

Moments flashing, a kaleidoscope,
Tangled up in a web of hope.
Days spin forth, a carnival ride,
Hold on tight, let fate decide.

Harmonizing with Life's Twists

A serenade sung in mismatched tunes,
Stepping on toes while waltzing with spoons.
Every twist is a chance to groove,
Who knew surprise could make me move?

Dancing through all the unexpected,
With socks that fight and shoes that rejected.
Laughter greets the missteps I make,
In this dance, let joy awake.

Tracing the Silhouette of Hope

In a world of shapes we roam,
Chasing shadows, never home.
Laughter hides behind each bend,
Waving flags that twist and blend.

When fortune slips and fate is sly,
We juggle dreams where giggles lie.
A cartoon heart with googly eyes,
Whispers tales of sweet surprise.

A starlit path, a comical fate,
We dance with clouds, while ducks ask 'Wait!'
Spin around, take care to trip,
On rubber bands and friendship's grip.

So hold on tight and lose that frown,
Together high, we'll never drown.
For in our hearts, we paint a scope,
Of every giggle that crowns our hope.

Sunlight After the Rain

Raindrops gallop on the street,
Puddles like mirrors, quite the feat.
Umbrellas flipped, a vibrant dance,
Wet socks squeak, oh what a chance!

Sun peeks out, a cheeky grin,
A golden ray, where to begin?
Splatting mud, a joyful stain,
We celebrate our own hurricane.

We skip and hop, oh such a joy,
With splashes loud, we each deploy.
Clouds giggle, they know our game,
As nature smiles, it feels the same.

And when the thunders laugh and cry,
We paint rainbows in the sky.
A joke from nature, rain or shine,
It's a wacky, happy, funny line.

The Pause Before the Storm

A stillness stirs, a vibrant hush,
Caught in a dance, we almost crush.
The air is thick, a playful tease,
Like cats on roofs ready to sneeze.

Suspense that hangs, a fizzy pop,
We're waiting for the chaos to drop.
A tick-tock clock with wobbly hands,
Balancing dreams on shaky stands.

A sudden gust, bright signs unmade,
Twisting leaves in wobbly parade.
Then laughter breaks like crackling waves,
At thunder's call, we act like knaves.

So here's to the pause, a child's delight,
With giggles echoing into the night.
We sip our tea, a storm in tow,
And grin at the winds that dare to blow.

Shadows of a Forgotten Dream

In the attic lies an old whim,
A blanket fort where dreams are grim.
Dust bunnies hop, they're quite the team,
Giving life to a wobbly scheme.

The whispers of wishes in moonlit beams,
Catch snippets of laughter, shred at the seams.
Old toys giggle in corners unseen,
As shadows dance in a playful sheen.

A butterfly net with holes in the side,
Trapping moments that now abide.
We summon ghosts of wishes past,
With silly hats—we know how to last.

So we raise a toast to the unseen plight,
With crooked grins in the pale moonlight.
For even shadows, in corners they bask,
Share secret laughs, if we only ask.

Secrets of the Quieted Heart

In whispers soft, a secret lies,
A heart that giggles, often sighs.
It dances gently through the day,
With all the things it can't quite say.

Like socks that vanish in the wash,
And moments sweeter than a posh.
It finds a laugh in every woe,
A tickled thought, a joy to show.

Pillow fights with shades of doubt,
Tickling fears that dance about.
A heart can play so many tricks,
Each thoughtful beat, a playful mix.

And when the sun starts to descend,
It hums a tune, your perfect friend.
For in the quiet, magic swirls,
In secrets kept from boys and girls.

Fleeting Wonders in Ordinary Time

Beneath the clock, the magic glows,
A toast to toast, and splashes, who knows?
In simple things, a dance occurs,
Life hands out spirals, and a few slurs.

The cat's wild pounce, the dog's slight bark,
Make ordinary turn to spark.
Each tick reminds us, 'Oh, surprise!'
Tomorrow's filled with silly highs.

Cupcakes wobble as they bake,
Life's mishaps hold a lot at stake.
Still, laughter bubbles, joy takes flight,
In fleeting wonders of the night.

So cheers to slip-ups, spills, and falls,
To singing loudly in the halls.
A wink, a laugh, as hours bloom,
In little wonders, find the room.

The Unseen Weavings of Tomorrow

Threads of laughter, woven tight,
In fabric soft, a bold delight.
Tomorrow teases, ever sly,
With quirky twists that make us cry.

The sock drawer yields its little prize,
A hanger's song beneath the skies.
Beneath the mundane, treasures gleam,
In stitches that unravel dreams.

Knots of fate, and tangled fate,
We trip on dreams, then back to straight.
Yet in the snags, humor shows,
In unseen weavings, the heart glows.

So open up your eyes, my dear,
There's wonder stitched throughout the year.
In playful knots, and tangled threads,
The joy of moments softly spreads.

Nuances of Surprise in Stillness

In quiet corners, a sneeze, a shout,
The silent giggles dance about.
A raised brow here, a smirk set free,
In stillness thick, we laugh with glee.

A hidden joke beneath a stare,
As time does twist, you're unaware.
Each pause a canvas, smiles unfold,
In subtle waves, their tales retold.

Life whispers secrets, soft and bright,
In silent laughter, day turns to night.
A glance, a nudge, a knowing grin,
In nuances, the fun begins.

So let us linger, savor the thrill,
In quiet moments, hearts can fill.
For surprise resides in gentle waits,
In stillness sweet, joy permeates.

Echoes of Breaths and Beyond

Woke up with a sock on my head,
Wondering how it got there instead.
The coffee spilled, the cat ran away,
Just another whimsical morning ballet.

I tripped on my shoelace, oh what a scene,
Chased by a dog or was it a dream?
The toast popped up with a mighty spring,
Burned and singing like it's trying to fling.

Whispers of the Unfolding Path

Walking forward, I bumped a tree,
Did it mean to stand there or just wanted to be?
A squirrel laughed, it made me grin,
Guess it knows where the fun begins.

Around the bend, I found a shoe,
Whose is it, and what did they do?
A twist of fate, or lost in the park,
I shrugged and laughed, it left a mark.

The Tapestry of Sudden Turns

Sometimes I'd sing, and pigeons would stare,
Did they critique or just didn't care?
Each twist and turn a jolly surprise,
Caught off-guard by a pie in the skies.

I danced with a broom, it was quite a sight,
As it swept the floor, we twirled with delight.
In the middle of chaos, I found my groove,
Life's a funny dance, just feel the move.

Breathless Moments

A sneeze in the middle of a grand speech,
Turning red and my words out of reach.
The audience chuckled, a merry brigade,
I laughed too, what a funny charade.

Found a penny on the sidewalk today,
Picked it up, then tossed it away.
Superstitions say it brings good cheer,
But not when I tripped on my last beer!

Serendipitous Turns

I opened the fridge and found a surprise,
A half-eaten cake that caught my eyes.
Forgotten treasures from yesterday's fun,
With a fork in hand, I dove right in, yum!

At the park, a bird stole my snack,
Feathers flew, and I had to crack.
Chasing it down like a silly racquet,
Who knew snacks could lead to such a racket?

Heartstrings in Cacophony

A cat on a keyboard strays,
While socks mysteriously fade.
We juggle our hopes and dreams,
Like clowns in a circus parade.

The phone rings, it's quite the surprise,
It's grandma with news of her pies.
Yet instead of warm, tasty treats,
She's sold them all—what a demise!

We dance in a whirl of delight,
While fortune teases from afar.
But missing keys come into view,
Just like that bizarre guitar.

With laughter that tickles our hearts,
We embrace each twist and each bend.
For in this mess, there's charm, you see,
A cacophony we won't end.

A Map of Hidden Delights

Morning coffee, a little too hot,
My face after the first sip—a plot!
Buried treasures of crumbs abound,
Under the couch in a tightly wedged knot.

Can you believe the socks that I find?
Each toe in the lost ones is blind!
The cat's now a treasure map,
Leading me to snacks he's combined.

Under the desk, a sandwich appears,
Forgotten for days, it brings me to tears.
The surprise of a taste, stale yet bold,
Turns my laughter into loud cheers!

With each twist and turn of our fate,
We stumble through joy, never late.
For in these little moments we see,
The map to delight is our fate.

Embracing the Uninvited

Unexpected guests come to play,
With quirks that brighten the gray.
At dinner, they spill the dessert,
But laughter's the best soufflé!

A dog steals the cake from the dish,
As wishes come true with a swish.
Life's uninvited antics unfold,
Like magic from a savory fish.

When the doorbell rings, I wonder who?
Perhaps a neighbor with cats to woo.
But it's just my friend with a tune,
That makes all my worries skew.

We toast to the absurdity here,
Cheers to the wild, far and near.
In chaos, there's joy, don't you know?
With laughter, we hold dear.

The Dance of Sighs and Revelations

A sneeze in a quiet room,
Turns heads and sparks quite the boom.
Revelations come with each sigh,
Like finding a flower in full bloom.

The socks do the tango and sway,
In the drawers where they long to play.
They slip and slide, just like us,
Making a game out of dismay.

As plans crumble like fragile glass,
We laugh more at each silly pass.
With secrets shared and tales to spin,
We'll dance through the future's vast grass.

So we sway to the rhythm of fate,
With chuckles that we cultivate.
In this waltz of quirks, we find our glee,
In every sigh and twist of slate.

Heartbeats in Unexpected Places

In the fridge, a mouse dances on cheese,
A beat so odd, it brings me to my knees.
Jellybeans roll like a carnival ball,
And laughter erupts from the bathroom stall.

The cat has a secret; she's wearing a hat,
She struts like a queen, but she's really a brat.
Forks and spoons play tag on the kitchen floor,
Who knew that cutlery could be such a bore?

An umbrella's plotting a rain dance tonight,
While socks mysteriously take off in flight.
The toaster pops toast like a fireworks show,
And I can't help but giggle at all of it, though.

So here's to the moments that catch us off guard,
Like clowns in the park or a runaway card.
May joy surprise us with quirks of the day,
And may our wild hearts forever stay play!

The Art of Letting Go

A balloon slips away, floating high in the sky,
And I can't help but wave, as it bids me goodbye.
Fridges of leftovers that gather some dust,
I open their doors, and I laugh, that's a must!

Old shoes in the closet that scream to be free,
"Take us to the beach!" They plead, "Can't you see?"
I toss out my worries with yesterday's bread,
While my plants start a riot, it's chaos instead.

A cat pawing at shadows, thinking it's prey,
The dust bunnies giggling, just taking their stay.
I grab my old jacket which once fit just right,
But it hugs me like guilt, and I laugh at the sight.

So here's to the clutter we gently release,
To letting things go, finding moments of peace.
May each little chuckle take flight on the breeze,
And life teach us softly the art of great ease!

Gentle Currents of Change

A goldfish swims circles, with dreams in his bowl,
He keeps to his path but wants to be whole.
But then there's the cat, inking plans on the rug,
He yearns to be free, or just give a hug.

Leaves leap from trees like they're dancing a jig,
The wind sings sweet nothings to each little twig.
With change comes the humor, like socks in a wash,
When one goes astray, the other just doth squosh.

The clock ticks in rhymes that are silly and loud,
While pancakes flip flopped, making breakfast quite proud.
Bananas start slipping in a dance out of tune,
While I trip on my thoughts under the light of the moon.

So let's laugh at the shifts that keep us awake,
The wiggles and giggles, and old rules we break.
May change be a joke, ever pleasingly strange,
As we ride on the waves of these gentle exchanges!

Fragments of a Flickering Dream

A rubber duck chorus, they sing by the sink,
Each note is a giggle, all pink on the blink.
They launch into waltzes, splash goggles in cheer,
As I float through the bubbles, my worries disappear.

The moon's throwing parties, dressed up like a star,
On nights when the awkward just dances too far.
While shoelaces tangle in interpretive art,
I'm merrily twisting, not pulled apart!

Mismatched socks whisper their plans to unite,
In the dryer, they plot a great escape from the night.
With cereal spilling, a backsplash of cheer,
I revel in chaos, my life is quite clear.

So here's to the dreams that are silly and bright,
To fragments of whimsy that dance in the light.
May we savor each moment as treasures on stream,
In the laughter of cracks, we'll find our own theme!

The Breath Between Moments

In the pause of a sneeze, oh what a thrill,
Tickle of fate, makes time stand still.
A cat on the prowl, just took a leap,
While I drop my ice cream, down the steep.

A wink from the universe, so sly and quick,
Just when you think it, it plays a trick.
You trip on a sidewalk, it's funny, I swear,
But laughter bubbles up, floating in air.

The clock's counting down, to an awkward dance,
A slip and a slide, will you take a chance?
Juggling life's lemons, with a twist of lime,
Finding joy in the chaos, isn't that sublime?

So hold your breath tight, for a giggle or two,
Between every moment, surprises renew.
When we least expect it, laughter appears,
A reminder that joy can outshine our fears.

Unraveled Threads of Tomorrow

The weather man says, it's sunny all day,
Yet I step outside, and it's pouring, hooray!
Umbrellas upside down, oh what a scene,
Chasing the raindrops, what could have been.

A sock lies misplaced, nowhere to be found,
One foot in sneakers, and one in the ground.
With mismatched attire, I strut down the street,
Unraveled threads make my day feel complete.

Puddles become dance floors, with splashes galore,
The world is a canvas; let's paint with uproar.
Missteps and mishaps, they weave as they go,
Creating a quilt of the warmth we all know.

So spin the wheel, with glee and delight,
In the fabric of tomorrow, surprises ignite.
Sewing smiles and chuckles, one stitch at a time,
In the unraveling dance of life's sweet rhyme.

When Laughter Hides in Shadows

In the corner of dusk, where giggles retreat,
Whispers of joy play a game of hide and seek.
A shadow sneezes, startled me too,
And suddenly everything seems less askew.

Behind every frown, there's a chuckle in wait,
Carrots on diets, oh isn't that great?
Running after dreams, we trip on our might,
Because who needs to fly when we float in delight?

A jester's old hat, thrown high to the eaves,
Catches the sunlight, then dances with leaves.
Fangless old monsters, with stories to share,
Brush off the cobwebs, let laughter declare!

So peek into shadows, let giggles unfold,
In the light of the moon, watch dreams turn to gold.
With a wink of surprise, the night comes alive,
In this carnival dance, we all shall survive.

Serendipity's Gentle Taps

A knock at the door, who could that be?
Oh, it's just my shoe, trying to break free!
Each twist and each turn, it's a comedic fate,
When socks have discussions, it's never too late.

The spoon in the drawer wished to dismay,
When a fork gets too sassy, say 'Not today!'
Chasing after giggles, we fumble and fall,
Like marbles in pockets, we hear the call.

Dropped my keys again, where could they be?
They prefer to hide, oh don't you agree?
A wild scavenger hunt, around the whole house,
Turns into a circus, just me and a mouse.

So smile with the universe, as it flat-out claps,
For serendipity's whispers, those gentle taps.
In the chaos of mischief, joy finds a way,
With a wink from the cosmos, we'll dance and play.

Portraits of Memory in the Wind

A squirrel stole my snack and ran,
Chased by a kite that just won't land.
Memories spin like a crazy dance,
As I trip over dreams in a silly trance.

I wore mismatched socks on a sunny day,
Thought it was fashion, they laughed anyway.
My heart was a drum, beating on time,
But my shoes were squeaking, oh what a mime!

A cat in a hat looked quite amused,
As I fumbled through life, slightly confused.
Each number I dial, an accidental prank,
Laughing with ghosts in my rusty tank.

Yet in all the chaos, joy finds a way,
In the tender moments, I struggle and sway.
So here's to the pictures that drift on by,
In the portraits of memory, we laugh and sigh.

Serendipitous Serenades

In a coffee shop, I spilled my drink,
A stranger laughed, and gave me a wink.
We talked of cats, and then of pies,
And sang out loud to the evening skies.

I found a penny, wished for a boat,
But ended up using it for a note.
The mailman grinned, he knows my game,
Sending post to the wind, never the same.

Two socks in the dryer, but one goes rogue,
It wanders the world, a fearless vogue.
Finding joy in items that sneak from the fold,
Each surprise is a story waiting to be told.

So let's raise a glass to the odd and bizarre,
In the serendipitous lives, we all are a star.
For every mishap, there's laughter and cheer,
In melodies playful, we have nothing to fear.

The Space Between the Notes

A band played loudly in the town square,
I danced like a fool, without a care.
Guitar strings tangled like my thoughts,
In the spaces between, joy is caught.

I missed my bus, it drove on past,
Made a new friend whose laugh was a blast.
We started a conga line down the street,
With each silly step, we felt so complete.

Life's unexpected, a curious tune,
Like singing with cats under a bright moon.
The awkward moments, we cherish and find,
Are the hidden cadences that leap to our mind.

So let's sway with the rhythm, embrace every blur,
Celebrate hiccups, and every sweet slur.
In the space between notes, let hearts intertwine,
In the dance of the quirky, we brightly shine.

Shattered Expectations and New Beginnings

I planned a picnic, it rained instead,
But underneath the porch, I baked some bread.
A squirrel joined me, sharing my seat,
With crumbs flying 'round, it turned out sweet.

Got lost on my way to the big city fair,
Ended up at a farm, with cows to stare.
Learned to juggle eggs with a rooster's cheer,
For all my missteps, I gained a new peer.

Each plan I set seems to fray at the seams,
But laughter resounds like a chorus of dreams.
What's broken can mend, a puzzle retained,
In the chaos and jests, new joys are gained.

So here's to the moments that stray from the norm,
To bouncing ideas and laughter's warm charm.
For every expectation that tumbles and spins,
There's a new beginning where the fun never thins.

Unraveled Threads of Fate

In a world of tangled threads,
I found my socks mismatched again.
Grapes in my pocket instead of lunch,
Oh, where do these little mishaps begin?

A cat stole my chair, oh the nerve!
Claiming it with a regal stance.
I laughed so hard, I lost my place,
And now I'm stuck in a cat-induced trance.

The coffee spilled right on my shirt,
Like an artist's stroke, it's quite a flair.
A chuckle escapes, I can't quite help,
These quirky moments, we all must share.

So here I dance on fate's funny line,
With gaps and twists woven keen.
A giggle, a sigh, a snack-sized joke,
These silly sorrows are truly serene.

The Sigh Between Heartbeats

Between each heartbeat lies a tale,
Of missed buses and ice cream falls.
With a sigh, I ponder, was it fate?
Or just my careless, goofy sprawl?

I tripped on air, what a clever trick,
A slip, a slide, oh so grand.
The crowd erupts—laughter truly,
Life's comedy carved in clumsy strands.

I bought a plant, it looked so grand,
But named it 'Tim', now he's turning brown.
My best friend laughs, "Just give it time!"
Oh, the irony, green thumbs I drown!

In the spaces between my sighs,
Lies comedy in every little crack.
With laughter as the thread that binds,
These heartbeats dance, no turning back.

Whispers of What Might Have Been

Once I pondered paths untaken,
Ordering what should never align.
A hat that fit my head just right,
Was actually a bumblebee's design.

Confetti fell from nowhere fast,
I stood befuddled in a toast.
The party's joy, alive and loud,
Left me a chuckler, but who gets the most?

I planned a trip, missed the flight,
Ended up launching my own taco stand.
With tacos tight and laughter loud,
What might have been is now unplanned.

In whispers soft, the stories weave,
Of mischief born from every chance.
Sighs and giggles, oh what a blend,
In laughter, I happily prance.

Journeys Uncharted: Sighs at Dusk

As the sun dips down, colors play,
I chase after moments, oh what a race.
Lost in a daydream, humor unfolds,
With fireflies laughing in dusk's embrace.

I took the wrong turn, what a plot twist,
Led me to ice cream instead of the store.
A symphony of flavors, you won't believe,
Sighs turn to giggles, who could ask for more?

I met a dog with a curious tail,
Who stole my shoelace and ran off, oh dear!
Chasing after him, I lost my way,
Yet in the trail of smiles, I had no fear.

In journeys that twist and meander loud,
Each sigh carries a jest on its breeze.
With stars like laughter lighting the path,
This uncharted dance sways with such ease.

Joy in the Unlikely Places

A cat in a hat sings loud and clear,
While ducks wear bow ties, oh what a cheer!
A fish in a bowl throws a wild little party,
And everyone dances, oh isn't that hearty?

In the depths of a shoe, a party was found,
With mice on the tables, all dancing around.
They sip tiny tea and munch on crumbs,
Who knew such joy came from fuzzy little chums?

An old man in slippers twirls like a sprite,
He juggles with apples, a comical sight.
His grin is contagious, spreads laughter anew,
Each chuckle erupts, like confetti it flew!

So seek out the magic in odd little scenes,
In the giggles of squirrels or the joy of machines.
For laughter erupts in the most quirky ways,
And happiness blooms in the simplest plays.

Echoes of Laughter in the Dark

In the depths of the night, shadows creep and crawl,
Yet giggles and chuckles echo through the hall.
A ghost with a grin shares a laugh with the moon,
While owls in tuxedos break out a soft tune.

A bat doing ballet swings low to the floor,
With a wink and a jig, he dances for more.
The frogs in tuxes croak a very loud joke,
And even the trees start to giggle and poke.

The stars twinkle back like they joined in the fun,
With a sparkle or two, they shine just for one.
So if you hear laughter when shadows grow long,
It's just the night's magic, a whimsical song!

In darkness, we find the bright and the bold,
With laughter that dances, a sight to behold.
So fear not the night, for it's filled with delight,
Just listen for joy that can brighten your plight.

The Slow Unfolding of Secrets

A box that won't open, a riddle, and fuss,
With whispers of secrets that giggle and cuss.
Each time you pry open that locked, heavy door,
A sock puppet shouts, 'You're not getting more!'

The cat in the corner has something to say,
With dramatic flair, she steals all the play.
In one paw, a clue, in the other, a snack,
She ponders her moves, then goes for the hack.

Frog hats and capes dance on the edge of your mind,
As revelations come wrapped in sticky gum find.
The secrets are silly, yet oh, what a thrill,
Each giggle unveils a new twist to the will.

So when life's little mysteries seem hard to unwrap,
Remember the gags and the laughter they tap.
For in every odd secret, a chuckle does dwell,
Waiting in shadows, a whimsical spell.

Notes from an Untold Journey

With boots made of rubber, I set out the door,
And tripped on a pebble while craving for more.
My map was a scribble, directions a jest,
Yet laughter soon found me, and won every quest.

I met a wise hedgehog who offered me tea,
While squirrels in jackets debated with glee.
They formed little teams, by tree trunk and leaf,
And laughed at my fumbles with no hint of grief.

The skies turned to candy, each cloud a delight,
As I stumbled and giggled in sheer, silly flight.
Every turn held a treasure, and each wrong way led,
To laughter that echoed, and joy that was spread.

So here's to the journeys that twist and that bend,
Where joy greets the lost and the silly pretend.
Embrace all the wonders, let laughter ignite,
For adventure is sweeter when shared in the light!

Surprises Beneath the Surface

In the shallow end, I take a dive,
A splash of joy makes me feel alive.
The pool is warm, but then I see,
A rubber duck staring back at me.

Beneath the waves, a treasure hides,
A sock from winter, it surely glides.
With each stroke, mysteries appear,
Like salad dressing when I want a beer!

Floating toys and rogue flip-flops,
In murky depths, the laughter never stops.
I swim with glee, embraced by the jest,
As the sun glitters on my blown-up vest.

Bubbles rise with a giggle and twist,
From the funny fish I can't resist.
All these quirks churn my thoughts haywire,
Who knew surface joys could take me higher?

The Melody of Unseen Journeys

Underneath the table, a cat plays drums,
With sticky keys and tiny thumbs.
The sofa's a boat, the rug is the sea,
Set sail for snacks, just my cat and me.

Outside the window, a bird does sing,
Like a rock star flapping his wing.
But wait! A squirrel hops by in a dance,
He gives me a wink, should I join the prance?

My travels begin with a click and a zoom,
From the couch to the fridge, it's my living room.
With a bowl of popcorn as my trusty map,
Adventure awaits, let's close the gap!

Moments like these bring a chuckle so bright,
As shadows of mischief ignite each night.
With each unseen path I serendipitously find,
A sitcom unfolds, future's kind!

Shadows Stretched by Daylight

With the morning sun, I'm a giant in play,
My shadow competes, what a raucous display!
I chase it round, what a silly sight,
With each leap, it tries to take flight.

On this road where shadows collide,
A dancing figure, with no place to hide.
The breeze brings whispers of sun-tanned glee,
My shadow and I are just wild and free.

A quick hop, a skip, oh what fun!
Dodging the light till the day's almost done.
In the afternoon, close friends draw near,
A game of tag, with laughter and cheer.

At dusk shadows shrink, bidding us bye,
A moment of smiles before they sigh.
From short to tall, a comedy show,
What a life it seems, only shadows know!

Serene Moments Amidst Chaos

Amidst the whirl of socks and shoes,
I find a teacup with hues of blues.
In the kitchen, a dance with pots and pans,
While my dog holds court, with snacks in his hands.

The world's a circus, and I'm the clown,
While spaghetti o'clock comes crashing down.
Juggling chores with a wink and a smile,
Laughter echoes through every trial.

When chaos rules, I take a pause,
Finding magic in the little flaws.
A moment of zen as laundry spins,
In the final act, the quirkiness wins.

So here's to calm amidst the ruckus,
The silly moments, oh so contagious.
For in every twist and small surprise,
Lies joy and giggles, vast as the skies!

Riding the Waves of Surprise

Oh, the ups and downs we ride,
Like a boat on a wobbly tide.
One moment a cheer, next a flinch,
Dodging mischief like it's a pinch.

Unexpected guests at dawn's ray,
Dance through the kitchen, hip-hip-hooray!
Burnt toast, spilled milk, laughter so loud,
Who knew chaos could draw a crowd?

A pie in the face, oh what a sight,
Life's little jests bringing delight.
Juggling dreams like plates on a stick,
One drop and the whole lot goes quick!

So grab your surfboard, join the fun,
Ride out the waves until day is done.
With giggles and gasps, we navigate,
Every surprise becomes a new fate.

Tides of Change and Stillness

In the quiet, the waves do crash,
Yet all around, there's a bash!
From serene tea sips to wild bops,
Life flips the script with its hops.

Where dull moments seem to dwell,
A phone call brings surprises as well.
Like socks that argue in the dryer,
Change here feels like a live wire!

One day you're a couch potato,
Next, you're dancing like a tornado.
Staying still may not be the key,
Who knew the calm could be so funny?

So embrace the swirl and whirl and spin,
Every twist leads to the next grin.
In the tides of change, oh what a scene,
Waves crash over while we sip on green.

The Gentle Pull of Contradiction

With a wink, the world spins 'round,
In contradictions, we're often found.
To be wise yet act like a fool,
It's a circus, and we're the fuel.

Jumping fences and rolling in dew,
Should we laugh when we should be blue?
Jumping from logic into a jest,
Life's sweet irony is the best!

Run for cover, oh what a plot,
But under umbrellas, we find what's sought.
We crave the wild yet seek the tame,
Contradictions whisper and play a game.

So hold this riddle close to heart,
Embrace the chaos, it's an art!
In every twist, a giggle's near,
In contradiction, we find our cheer.

Ripples in a Still Pond

In a pond that seems so calm,
A pebble drops, brings a qualm.
Those quiet moments may not hold,
The laughter hidden, tales to be told.

With ripples dancing on the surface,
A splash of joy, here comes the circus!
Expecting stillness, get a surprise,
Fish trying to wear a bowl full of ties!

Sitting still with a cup of tea,
Yet a frog jumps right next to me.
As tranquil thoughts meet playful glee,
Life throws splashes so carelessly!

So here's to ponds and their little tricks,
And finding fun in all of life's picks.
With every ripple, a giggle blooms,
Watch out for joy in all the rooms!

Curves of Fate and Gentle Echoes

Woke up today, thought I'd be great,
But tripped on my shoelace, oh what a fate!
Coffee's too hot, it spills on my shirt,
Guess my morning's just begging for hurt.

Barked like a dog when I saw my old friend,
He laughed so hard, was that the end?
Life serves up jokes on a silver tray,
Who knew happiness hid in dismay?

Can't find my keys, they're lost in the fray,
My cat's having fun, in her own little way.
She leaps like a ninja, just misses the chair,
Now I'm giggling, but I can't help but stare.

Is it empty fridge or a surprise snack?
Each moment unfolds; I fall off track.
With a chuckle and sigh, I ride the trend,
In this clumsy waltz, there's joy to mend.

The Dance of Joy and Regret

I wore mismatched socks, what a bold choice,
A look that says, 'Does this outfit rejoice?'
Yet strutting my stuff, oh the looks I got,
Turns out my fashion just can't hit the spot.

Dinner burned down, I tried to impress,
My date laughed so hard, what a glorious mess!
We toasted to failures over burnt spaghetti,
In the dance of our hearts, we felt so ready.

Forgot my umbrella on such a wet day,
The sky laughed hysterically, made me its prey.
Drenched to the bone, I danced down the street,
With joy in my steps, I couldn't accept defeat.

A chat with a stranger over frozen fries,
He told me a joke that brought tears to my eyes.
In the rhythm of mishaps, we twirl and sway,
In a comedy reel, we find our own way.

Fluctuations in the Breath of Time

Alarm goes off, but I hit snooze quick,
Dreaming of tacos, oh what a trick!
Time skips ahead, like a playful sprite,
Now I'm late for work, oh this isn't right.

At the bus stop, I tripped on a shoe,
Landed in laughter, like what do I do?
A stranger paused, gave me a grin,
In this whirlwind of chaos, we both fit in.

Checked my phone, messages piled high,
"Did you forget?" Yes, oh me, oh my!
Life's little reminders flashing too bright,
But with every mishap, a giggle ignites.

Chasing the sunset, with splashes of light,
Each moment's a punchline, a dance in the night.
In the swings of the clock with its tick-tock chime,
We find our serenity in the breath of time.

Harmonies in the Unexpected

Found a sock in the fridge, what a surprise,
Guess I'll start a trend, oh how time flies!
My cereal escaped, it took a huge leap,
In the bowl of confusion, I tripped on a sweep.

Wandering the mall, lost track of my crew,
Followed a kid with ice cream, what else to do?
We ended in laughter in a candy store,
Life's sweet surprises knock at every door.

Old love letters turned into paper planes,
Flying high above with all their refrains.
Each fold tells a story, of joy and despair,
In a flight of fancy, we discover repair.

So let's embrace the quirks, the snags, and the falls,
In the symphony of moments, laughter calls.
With echoes of wonder in all that we do,
Let's dance to the tune, it's silly but true.

Cascading Moments of Truth

Monday morning slips away,
Coffee spills, what a display.
Chasing thoughts that drift and fly,
Just can't remember why, oh why.

A rubber chicken meets a cat,
In the drawer, imagine that.
Tickling giggles, jumbled noise,
Surprises hide in mundane joys.

Traffic lights, they love to tease,
Red and green, none seem to please.
A walk on eggshells, oh so fun,
How did I end up on the run?

A toaster with a mind of its own,
Burnt toast and laughter overthrown.
Every twist a chance to grin,
What's next, a dance-off with a pin?

In-Between the Happenstance

A sock goes missing, what a prank,
Washing machine's a sneaky tank.
Dancing dust bunnies sing a tune,
Under the bed, they plot by moon.

Snakes and ladders on a busy street,
Feet stumble over unexpected feet.
A pigeon struts, claims his ground,
At a picnic, he steals the sound.

Unexpected calls from distant friends,
Gossip that just never ends.
A laugh erupts from deep inside,
In every hiccup, joy will glide.

Wobbly chairs with stories to tell,
A cupcake emerges, who'd guess so well?
Life's random play, a vibrant scene,
Tomorrow's blues in lemon sheen.

The Pulse of the Unpredictable

A squirrel steals snacks with glee,
In a tree, laughing at me.
Unexpected drop, a sudden twist,
Dish soap bubbles, say what's this?

A hat flies off on blustery days,
Twirling round in vast ballet.
Laughter echoes in the park,
Even the trees hum their own spark.

Jelly beans jump from the jar,
Rolling fast, they travel far.
Chasing treats, we take a bow,
Who knew sweets could teach us how?

Giggles spring from every nook,
Every glance, a funny look.
With silly moments woven tight,
Surprises dance in morning light.

Fleeting Shadows of Tomorrow

A shadow dances in the sun,
Only to vanish, oh what fun.
Tickling toes on sandy shores,
As waves come in, and laughter roars.

An umbrella flips, the rain begins,
Chasing ducks and fateful spins.
A frog in a top hat croaks a rhyme,
Wishing we could freeze this time.

The clock strikes noon, it's pancake day,
Flipping flops in a pancake array.
We juggle childhood on a whim,
And friendship grows, though chances seem slim.

What's next, an alien on a bike?
Claiming the road, oh what a hike!
Through every twist, we find delight,
In fleeting moments, laughter takes flight.

Notes on the Wind's Whimsy

A gust blew my hat away,
It danced like a bird on a sunny day.
Chasing it down, a sight to behold,
I tripped on a twig, oh, how I rolled!

The breeze tickles leaves, such playful sounds,
As I search for my hat on the cold, hard grounds.
A squirrel eyed me with a knowing grin,
Guess even nature finds humor within!

My shoes are a mess, mud-streaked with flair,
A ballet of blunders in midair.
But laughter erupts when I finally see,
My hat on a dog's head? Oh, what glee!

So here's to the whims of a teasing wind,
It shows us laughter when we least intend.
With every surprise that tosses our way,
Let's giggle and sigh, come what may!

Expectation's Gentle Disappointment

I planned a picnic with sandwiches neat,
Imagined the sun, the fresh air so sweet.
But clouds rolled in, with a thunderous pout,
Our loaf turned into a soggy sprout!

We laughed at the drizzle; umbrellas went up,
Sipping on drinks from a broken cup.
Ants held their meeting on my potato salad,
A feast for them, our plans slightly salad!

"Next time," we said, "it'll surely be fine,
No rain in our future, just sunshine divine."
But life, oh so funny, threw lemons in tow,
Lemonade dreams in a rain-soaked show!

So here's to missteps that twist and confound,
To lessons in humor, even when drowned.
For in every blunder, a joy can be found,
Through puddles and giggles, we dance all around!

A Symphony of Sudden Winds

A breeze plays a tune, unexpected surprise,
I nearly flipped over, much to my demise.
With papers a-flying and hats in the air,
A clumsy conductor leading the fair!

Neighbors peek out, with coffee in hand,
Watching my chaos, it's comedy grand.
A masterpiece painted in chaos and cheer,
With every gust laughter draws near!

My shirt flaps like flags in a powerful storm,
Yet I pirouette, feeling oddly warm.
The wind's little winks, oh what a delight,
Turns fumbles to giggles, making it right!

So let's weave through the day with a skip and a prance,
Embrace every moment, take fate in a dance.
For even when life flings us out for a spin,
We'll laugh loud together, our symphony's win!

Tides of Hope and Hesitance

The waves roll in, bringing dreams on the shore,
I reach for a shell, find a sock, nothing more.
Yet there's joy in the odd, if only we see,
What treasures await, just waiting for me!

With hopes in my pocket and sand in my toes,
I shout at the seagulls, they mock like old pros.
Nature's a comedian, pulling my leg,
Each joke pulls a smile, no need for a peg!

Yet when the tide pulls back, and seaweed won't budge,
I laugh at the jumbles, they give me a nudge.
For each little surprise, each twist of fate,
Becomes a part of the story; oh, isn't that great?

So here's to the moments of giggles and grins,
In tides of uncertainty, laughter begins.
With hope in our hearts and a wink from the skies,
Let's dance through the moments, where laughter will rise!

Wrinkles in the Fabric of Existence

Fate's sewing machine hums loud,
It stitches quirks into the shroud.
Every pluck a giggle, each tear a yelp,
In this quilt of chaos, we find our help.

Threads unravel, but they weave anew,
A sweater here, a scarf or two.
Giggling at blunders, we dance along,
In this fabric of folly, we all belong.

Laughter ensues from a button's pop,
As we tumble through, we never stop.
Wrinkles in wisdom, crinkles of cheer,
Embrace the oddness, hold it near.

So don your patterns with flair today,
Every mistake is a curious play.
Tangles and knots, they'll surely constrict,
But in this odd weaving, souls connect.

Riddles of Change and Constancy

In the garden of time, we plant and sow,
Yet weeds of change always seem to grow.
Hats on and off, economies swing,
With every twist, a tune we sing.

Predict the forecast, but it rains instead,
We dance in mud till we're thoroughly thread.
A constant surprise, like socks that don't pair,
In riddles of change, there's seldom a care.

Pick a flower, a puzzle to solve,
Expecting a rose, but who knows what's involved?
Laugh at the thorns, they bite and annoy,
Each bruise is a mark of a tangible joy.

So tiptoe on riddles, and trip down the lane,
Constancy's banner, it flaps in the rain.
Embrace the mischief that comes with the ride,
In the dance of change, let humor abide.

Whispers of the Unexpected

A chicken crossed, but why was it there?
To reach for the joke that hung in the air.
Whispers of humor slip through the cracks,
A banana peel waiting, ready to tax.

The spoon slips from grasp, it bounces and flings,
Turning casserole into a plate of springs.
Whimsy whispers softly, wrapping us tight,
In a world of the silly, we play through the night.

Dropped my phone, and oh what a sight—
The cat in mid-leap, a clumsy delight!
Videos play, capturing the zest,
In every mishap, there's laughter expressed.

So when things go awry, don't fret or despair,
Embrace the confusion, let it lay bare.
For whispers of oddness are treasures to find,
In a realm of surprises, we open our mind.

Echoes of Joy and Discontent

In the echoes of giggles, there's snorts of regret,
A pin goes pop in a world quite upset.
Joy tiptoes lightly, then steps on a rake,
In the chorus of chaos, we all get awake.

Fart jokes resound through the halls of the wise,
While wisdom confounds with these goofy surprise.
A dance of emotions, the happy and sad,
In the theater of living, oh isn't it mad?

Tears blend with chuckles, a tapestry fraught,
Like a bird that can't sing, but tries all that's taught.
Echoes of laughter, in shadows they play,
Bright moments spill forth in a comical way.

So navigate squabbles with grace and with glee,
In joy and discontent, there's humor to see.
Each echo reflects where the heart wants to lean,
In this game of existence, we laugh in between.

The Canvas of the Unforeseen

Colors splash in random glee,
A brush that dances, wild and free.
The sky throws fits, then wears a grin,
As giggles spill where dreams begin.

A canvas waits for every jest,
With paint-splattered feet, we do our best.
A smile carved in every swirl,
In this mad whirl, we twirl and twirl.

Splashes of green, a burst of red,
Accidents laugh, no rules to dread.
Each stroke a chuckle, every hue,
A masterpiece of bright debut.

Chaos reigns where whimsy sings,
With every drip, delight it brings.
So grab your brush, don't fear the spill,
For in the mess, we find the thrill.

Storms in Teacups

A teacup tips, a tempest brews,
Panic dances in tiny shoes.
Slightly stirred, yet wildly spent,
What a fuss, for just a dent!

A spoon falls in, a splash, a swirl,
What's the ruckus? Oh, the whirl!
We laugh while sipping, soaked in tea,
A storm within, but warm are we.

Laughter tumbles like sugar cubes,
As friends debate their teapot tubes.
"Oh dear me!" spills one with flair,
While others giggle, foam in hair!

A ruckus brewed, but safety's bright,
In our cups, the world feels right.
So let them storm, we hold our ground,
In every drop, joy can be found.

The Mystery of Winding Paths

Winding roads, a joke or two,
With every turn, a new view.
Lost in thought, a gag unfolds,
Around the bend, a story told.

Sidewalks twist, like a playful tease,
Step on a crack, a ticklish breeze.
A signpost winks, says, "Go the way!"
Calamity's dance leads us astray.

Each twist a plot, a chuckle bright,
Frogs on a signpost, what a sight!
Straying from paths we thought we knew,
Where mischief blooms, and fun is due.

So gather round, my friends, let's roam,
In every drift, we find our home.
For the journey's punchline is all that we need,
In winding trails, laughter is freed.

Notes from a Secret Diary

Open the lid, a secret burst,
Confessions spill, my heart rehearsed.
Bubbles of giggles, whispers of tears,
Ticklish tales of all my fears.

"A squirrel stole my sandwich today!"
What else can I mutter in this way?
Plans for romance, love notes all jumbled,
In crumpled pages, my thoughts unshuffled.

Each entry moans, "Oh what a fright!"
Then bursts into laughter, a pure delight.
Quirky dreams and silly schemes,
Scrawled in margins, bursting at seams.

So come, my muse, bring forth the quirk,
In messy margins where giggles lurk.
My diary holds the world's sweet charms,
Wrapped in notes, it cuddles in arms.

Laughter in the Midst of Woe

When Mondays feel like a slap in the face,
I trip on my shoelace, oh what a disgrace.
But with coffee in hand, I muster a grin,
Stumbling through chaos, I somehow begin.

Each mishap a chuckle, each blunder a cheer,
I laugh at my troubles, they all disappear.
A cat on my laptop, a dog in the way,
In this circus of flops, I'll dance through the day.

The toaster explodes, the eggs hit the floor,
I cackle and giggle, as I come back for more.
For in every slip, there's a joke yet to tell,
I embrace all the chaos, and bid it farewell.

So here's to the laughter, in moments of pain,
Like rain turning sunny, like joy after rain.
With each stumble and fall, a sweet punchline found,
In the funny side of life, we're humorously bound.

Encounters with the Unexpected

Round the corner, a llama, who'd have guessed?
Impromptu parade, I'm lightly stressed.
It's wearing a hat, like it owns the street,
I laugh at the turmoil, my day's quite the treat.

An umbrella takes flight in a gust of surprise,
Chasing it down, I feel oh-so-wise.
A child with a balloon, just too much to take,
We giggle together, our hearts we won't break.

Oh, the detours we take, like a winding old road,
An ice cream cone slips, watch the chaos explode!
With each twist and turn, a new story unfolds,
In these little surprises, our laughter beholds.

So bring on the llamas, the winds and the ice,
In every small mishap, there's something precise.
Encounters out of nowhere, what a delight,
With each sudden turn, we'll embrace the bright.

Journeys Lined with Uncertainty

I set out for coffee, got lost on my way,
Found a party instead, with games on display.
A dance-off with strangers, my rhythm's a flop,
But laughter escapes me, I'm never gonna stop.

A map in my hand, but the road's not quite clear,
I drive to find joy, but I end up in beer.
With each twist of fate, I clutch at my fate,
Serendipity giggles as I try to relate.

A missed bus, a weird train, that's how it goes,
I stumble on journeys, just nudged by my toes.
With friends made in chaos and smiles so wide,
Uncertainty dances, it's nothing to hide.

So let's toast to the travels; bring on the strange,
For in every wrong turn, there's room to exchange.
A journey's best told with a wink and a sigh,
With laughter so hearty, we're free to fly high.

Chronicles of the Unplanned

Oh, the day began with a simple old plan,
But winds of mischief, they surely began.
The eggs weren't quite cooked, the toast took a dive,
Yet here I am smiling, so glad I'm alive.

A stroll through the park? What a great idea!
Until a squirrel declares that it's time for a beer.
We share a quick laugh as he wiggles his tail,
In this world of the odd, we're always set sail.

Plans change like weather, from bright sun to rain,
But I'll twirl in the puddles, without any pain.
For every mishap is a story to tell,
In chronicles varied, we stumble through well.

So here's to the moments we never foresaw,
To the belly laughs loud, and the chaos we draw.
With surprises around, we'll treasure the fun,
In the unplanned adventures, we are always begun.

The Tapestry of Joy and Grief

In a world of chuckles, we all wear a grin,
Balloons bursting loudly, let the fun begin!
A tumble down stairs, a coffee that spills,
We gather our stories, like scattered little thrills.

With giggles and sobs, we dance in delight,
A circus of moments, both wrong and so right.
The jester in me loves to jive and to play,
Turns tears into laughter, chase the blues away.

A cake that's a flop, but hey, that's quite grand!
We blow out the candles, make wishes unplanned.
Through fumbles and blunders, we paint the scene,
A canvas of chaos, where we all reign supreme.

So here's to the gaffes, the slips that we take,
Each moment a stitch in this tapestry fake.
With smiles as our thread, and our hearts all aglow,
We weave through the mayhem, let merriment flow!

Hidden Treasures in the Mundane

Every mundane Monday, socks missing their mates,
A treasure hunt starts, it's never too late!
Under the couch, with crumbs and some dust,
We laugh at the chaos, in silliness trust.

Locked in the cupboard, a dust-covered game,
Who knew such a find could ignite such a flame?
A dance with the mop, while humming a tune,
We twirl through the chores, who needs the moon?

In the bottom of drawers, old photos collide,
Beaming with memories, our giggles abide.
A burnt casserole, but leftovers shine bright,
Dinner for champions, our boldest delight.

So here's to the treasures, both hidden and near,
In the simplest places, let's revel in cheer.
With laughter our compass, we stumble and roam,
In ordinary moments, we'll always feel home.

A Symphony of Shadows and Light

The shadows are silly, they wiggle and sway,
They play hide and seek, in a comical way.
A dance with the sunlight, a sparkling race,
When they trip over nothing, oh, the look on their face!

The moon rolls its eyes, as the stars start to hum,
While the clouds bring the giggles, oh, what a drum!
A symphony screeches, and laughter ignites,
As the sun throws a party, in its golden delights.

In a world of the wacky, shadows share jokes,
They slip on banana peels, those lighthearted folks.
With giggling flickers, they lighten the mood,
Turning serious moments into our best food.

So join in the chorus, where shadows remain,
Swaying and laughing in a joyful refrain.
The night may be dark, but it's filled with our cheer,
A symphony playing, let's all gather near!

The Unexpected Dance of Time

Tick-tock goes the clock, a mischievous tease,
With moments all jumbled, it dances with ease.
Like a cat on a treadmill, it fumbles away,
Making giggles erupt on a random Thursday.

Suddenly, it's Tuesday, but wait it's a dream,
We're jumping through hoops, just to giggle and gleam.
A calendar prank that always goes wrong,
But who needs a plan when we've got joyful song?

With birthdays that vanish, and seasons that skip,
We trip on the past, let hilarity rip.
The minutes are bouncy, like rubbery balls,
Each second a surprise, oh how time enthralls!

So here's to the moments we never expect,
To the dance that confuses, let's all disconnect.
With laughter as rhythm, and joy as the rhyme,
We twirl through the chaos, in this wacky time!

Fleeting Moments

A cup of coffee spills at dawn,
The cat's indifferent, just yawns on.
A sock lost in the laundry race,
And yet we laugh at time and space.

A sneeze at the wrong time can shock,
The neighbor's dog thinks he's a rock.
We trip on words and dance in shoes,
In moments fleeting, we find our clues.

Lasting Imprints

A pie on the windowsill takes a dive,
The dog licks it clean, oh what a jive!
A family feud over pizza slices,
Yet all is forgiven with sweet, cold ices.

The leaves swirl round, a tornado of cheer,
Caught in a shoe, they decide to adhere.
A stamp on the hand from a concert bold,
Reminds us of nights when the stories unfold.

A Kaleidoscope of Chance Encounters

A stranger trips over their own shoe,
They laugh with eyes bright, as bright as the blue.
Two buses collide in a twist of fate,
While waiting, we ponder on what makes us late.

The sun sets low on a clumsy dance,
As squirrels pursue a dubious chance.
A smile exchanged in a coffee shop line,
A moment like this feels perfectly fine.

The Kaleidoscope of Breath

A yawn sneaks out in a serious chat,
The room erupts, it's a laugh attack.
We watch the clock tick and tock like a show,
As we sip on our tea, where did the time go?

An awkward silence fills up the space,
When someone laughs with a splatter of grace.
We breathe in the chaos, sigh out the stress,
In this whimsical world, we find our best.

Steps Taken in Softest Silence

Tiptoe through life on invisible beams,
Creating new paths, chasing our dreams.
A whisper of joy floats on the breeze,
While we giggle soft, just like the leaves.

A misplaced shoe on the doorstep's end,
Leads to a story we love to send.
The echoes of laughter, a gentle refrain,
Reminds us again, it's all part of the game.

www.ingramcontent.com/pod-product-compliance
Lightning Source LLC
Chambersburg PA
CBHW051631160426
43209CB00004B/602